A Short and Sweet Introduction

to the

Great American West Vacation

a travel guide of tips and ideas based on my family's United States west road trip

Joe Dodridge
©2018

A Short and Sweet Introduction to the Great American West Vacation

Visit *www.shortandsweetintroductions.com/westlinks* for websites and resources

A Short and Sweet Introduction to the Great American West Vacation

a travel guide of tips and ideas based on my family's United States west road trip

www.shortandsweetintroductions.com

Copyright ©2018
ISBN: 9781983210259

All rights reserved. Don't copy it! You might have a cool haircut and I don't copy it. So, don't copy my book.

This book is for entertainment purposes. It is understood that things change all of the time and some information might be incomplete or inaccurate.

Cover image: my picture in Badlands National Park

Logo: modified from an image by David on https://commons.wikimedia.org/wiki/File:Handshake_by_David.svg

US Maps: modified with permission

A Short and Sweet Introduction to the Great American West Vacation

Visit *www.shortandsweetintroductions.com/westlinks* for websites and resources

Table of Contents

What is This Book? --- 7
The Trip in Two Pages -- 9
Map – Our Trip in a Nutshell -------------------------------- 11
Our Crazy Planning Spreadsheet ------------------------------ 12

OUR TRIP
Day 1 – Drive, Drive, Drive --------------------------------- 14
Day 2 – South Dakota --------------------------------------- 17
Honorable Mention – Black Hills National Forest ---------- 23
Day 3 – South Dakota, Wyoming, and Montana ----------- 27
Honorable Mention – Glacier National Park --------------- 32
Day 4 – Yellowstone National Park (1st Day) ------------- 33
Day 5 – Yellowstone National Park (2nd Day) ------------ 40
Honorable Mention – Grand Tetons, Salt Lake City and
   Zion National Park ------------------------------------- 45
Day 6 – Driving with a Stop by Lake Tahoe --------------- 47
Day 7 – San Francisco -------------------------------------- 50
Day 8 – Pacific Coast -------------------------------------- 53
Day 9 – Los Angeles --------------------------------------- 57
Day 10 – Disney California Adventure Park --------------- 60
Honorable Mention – More Los Angeles
   and San Diego -- 62
Day 11 – Driving and Las Vegas --------------------------- 64
Day 12 – Driving and Grand Canyon ---------------------- 66
Honorable Mention – Alternate Route Home through
   Canyonlands and Arches -------------------------------- 70
Day 13 – Mesa Verde and Driving ------------------------- 71
Day 14 – Drive, Drive Drive ------------------------------- 74

OTHER THINGS
A Word About Lodging -------------------------------------- 77
What is the Difference Between a National Park,
   National Monument, National Memorial, Etc.? --------- 78

Flying to Start Your Trip ------------------------------------- 79
Time of Year -- 80
Animals We Saw on Our Trip ------------------------------- 81
Other American West Trips ---------------------------------- 82
Other Resources --- 83
About the Author -- 85

SPECIAL TIP!!!

Visit

www.shortandsweetintroductions.com/westlinks

for links to the websites of each park and memorial, as well as other resources.

Visit *www.shortandsweetintroductions.com/westlinks* for websites and resources

What is This Book?

This is the book I wish I had!!!

A few years ago, our family went on a great American west road trip. We loaded up our kids (then 9 and 12 years old), a couple of grandparents, too many suitcases, and headed west.

Now, don't think we just winged it. I spent countless hours planning – reading, researching, calling, and asking. I talked to my parents who've been out west a few times. I talked to other people who've gone out west. I even relied on memories I had as a kid. But, what I didn't have was a book that told me "these are the places where you need to go and this is what you're going to see."

So, what is this book? This book is your introduction to the great American west vacation. The book will follow the two-week route we took, with some additional side-trip options thrown in.

This book isn't a book of stories, though it is our story. This book isn't an all-encompassing guide, though there are plenty of tips and suggestions.

This book is all of my research and experiences written down for you to plan your own trip.

Maybe you don't even know where to start. Where should you go? Does time of year matter? What are the main national parks? What's it like in the desert, the mountains, and the prairie? Is seeing redwood trees worth it (yes!)?

This is a brief book and won't go into every hotel and dining option. I'll give you basic information about each park and attraction, but you can learn more by visiting my website, www.shortandsweetintroductions.com/westlinks, for links to the websites of those parks and attractions.

This book is organized in the order that we took our trip – from Day 1 to Day 14. Scattered throughout the book are "Honorable Mentions" – brief sections of the book that describe places we didn't visit, but you might want to add to your trip.

At the end of the book is a section called "Other Things." Here you'll find overall hints and tips about lodging, learn the difference between national parks and monuments, and more.

So, pack your backs (figuratively) and get comfortable (literally), and let's go out west!

Visit *www.shortandsweetintroductions.com/westlinks* for websites and resources

The Trip in Two Pages

This trip covers a big loop of the western United States, starting in the north and ending in the south. It doesn't really matter where you start – our first attraction was in South Dakota. It also doesn't matter where you finish – our last attraction was in Colorado.

So, starting on I-90 in South Dakota, we visited the **Minuteman Missile National Historic Site**, **Badlands National Park**, **Wall Drug**, **Mt. Rushmore**, **Sturgis**, and **Deadwood**. There are other things to do here too (Crazy Horse Memorial, Wind Cave National Park, Jewel Cave National Monument, and Custer State Park) – they will get an honorable mention and you might decide to add them to your trip.

Heading west and slightly north, we visited **Devil's Tower** and **Little Bighorn National Monument**. An honorable mention from here is to head further north to Glacier National Park, though we didn't do it on our trip because of time.

Next, we dropped down into **Yellowstone National Park** where we spent two days, but you can actually take more than a week to appreciate this park!

Our trip from Yellowstone took us to San Francisco. Along the way (long and boring!) we took a detour by **Lake Tahoe**. It's worth mentioning that many peoples' west trips don't go to San Francisco, but rather drop south from Yellowstone to Grand Teton National Park and Utah. I'll mention those as an honorable mention, but this book doesn't take that route!

In San Francisco, we visited **Alcatraz**, **Fisherman's Wharf**, the **Golden Gate Bridge**, and took a bus tour (warning about bus tours: you get what you pay for!).

A Short and Sweet Introduction to the Great American West Vacation

Leaving San Francisco, we saw redwood trees in **Henry Cowell Redwoods State Park**, and drove the **Pacific Coast Highway** south towards Los Angeles.

In L.A., we went on a **Hollywood tour** and a **whale-watching tour**, went to the beach, and went to **Disney California Adventure Park**. Of course, there are other things in L.A. that we didn't do that deserve an honorable mention. And, although we didn't go to San Diego, I've been there before and will also mention that in the honorable mention.

From L.A., we drove east to Las Vegas. We didn't see anything in particular, but we did walk around and take in the sights (some sights you don't want your kids to see!).

Leaving Las Vegas (which is a movie I've never seen), we quickly saw the **Hoover Dam** and drove to the **Grand Canyon**. Then heading east, we visited **Mesa Verde National Park** and waved to the **Great Sand Dunes National Park** as we continued our way home. There are other options to head east from the Grand Canyon. I'll go over those options in an honorable mention (Utah's national parks with sights in Colorado or heading straight home through New Mexico).

We did this trip in 14 days, and while it was a little crazy, I'd do it all again! As you read this book, at times you'll wonder how we fit it all in and other times you'll think I'm an idiot for skipping over something on our trip.

Use our trip as a guide for your trip. No doubt you'll want to change it up, add and delete. And hey, if you have a full month, do it all – honorable mentions included!

Visit *www.shortandsweetintroductions.com/westlinks* for websites and resources

Map – Our Trip in a Nutshell

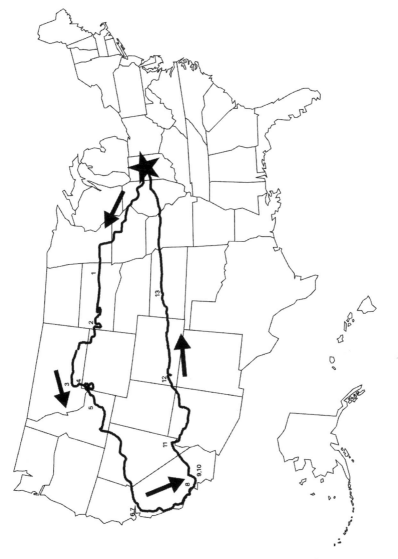

(numbers indicate where we spent that night)

A Short and Sweet Introduction to the Great American West Vacation

Our Crazy Planning Spreadsheet

Day	Miles	active hours	Itinerary	Night	
Saturday, July 2	1	765	15	drive/lunch (11), supper with family (2), drive (2)	Sioux Falls, SD	Clubhouse Hotel and Suites
Sunday, July 3	2	356	15	**we get 1 extra hour drive/lunch (5), Minuteman Missile (1), Badlands (3), Wall Drug/Supper (2), drive and check-in Lazy U (1.5), drive (.5), Mount Rushmore with lighting ceremony (1.5), drive (.5) **we get 1 extra hour	Rapid City, SD	Lazy U
Monday, July 4	3	527	13	drive (1), Deadwood (1), drive/lunch (2), Devil's Tower (1), drive/supper (4.5), Little Bighorn (1), drive (2.5)	Livingston, MT	Livingston Inn
Tuesday, July 5	4	163	13	Yellowstone (about 1 hour into Yellowstone)	Gardiner, MT	Super 8
Wednesday, July 6	5	269	13	Yellowstone (about 2 hours out of Yellowstone)	Fort Hall, ID	Shoshone-Bannock Hotel
Thursday, July 7	6	809	15	drive/lunch (10), supper at Lake Tahoe (1.5), drive (3.5) **note we get 1 extra hour	Dublin, CA	Hyatt Place Dublin/Pleasanton
Friday, July 8	7	0	12	sight see in San Francisco (take train in, trolley, Alcatraz, bus tour, Golden Gate Bridge)	Dublin, CA	Hyatt Place Dublin/Pleasanton
Saturday, July 9	8	386	12	drive coast and meals (about 7.5 hours of driving plus stops)	Westlake Village, CA	Hyatt Regency Westlake
Sunday, July 10	9	100	12	sight see in Los Angeles (bus in Hollywood: Chinese Theater & star sidewalk, Rodeo Drive; whale watching in Newport Beach)	Los Angeles	Best Western Plus Anaheim Inn
Monday, July 11	10	0	15	Disneyland - California Adventure (hours are 8-10, show at 10:15p)	Los Angeles	Best Western Plus Anaheim Inn
Tuesday, July 12	11	270	12	drive (4), sight see in Las Vegas (8) (Bellagio fountains, Fremont St., Mirage volcano, Treasure Island)	Las Vegas	Hyatt - New York, New York
Wednesday, July 13	12	554	13	drive/lunch (5), Grand Canyon (2), drive/supper (6) **note we lose one hour	Cortez, CO	White Eagle Inn and Lodge
Thursday, July 14	13	608	14.5	drive (.25), Mesa Verde (2), drive/lunch (4.75), Great Sand Dunes (1), drive/supper (6.5) **note we lose 1 hour	Oakley, KS	Kansas Country Inn
Friday, July 15	14	859	14.5	drive, drive, drive (12.5 hours driving) **note we lose 1 hour	home!	

12

Visit *www.shortandsweetintroductions.com/westlinks* for websites and resources

OUR TRIP

A Short and Sweet Introduction to the Great American West Vacation

Day 1 – Drive, Drive, Drive (765 miles)

The first day of your trip will probably be a lot like the first day of our trip – driving a long way just to start being out west!

Our trip took us out of Indianapolis, across Illinois, through Iowa, across the southern part of Minnesota and into Sioux Falls, South Dakota for our first night.

While today wasn't a sightseeing day, we did see three things that you might want to consider, depending on where you're coming from.

1. We stopped by **Antique Archaeology** in LeClaire, Iowa. Antique Archaeology is the home store of the television show *American Pickers*. The store is pretty small, but full of unique items that you can actually purchase. Don't expect to see anyone from the show hanging around! It's more of a tourist destination than a cool mom and pop place like the show implies.

2. We stopped by the **Iowa 80 Truck Stop** in Walcott, Iowa. It claims to be the world's largest truck stop. I don't know if it actually is or not, but this is exactly the kind of place that you think of when you think of a great American road trip. There are plenty of dining options and a bazillion things you can buy.

3. We ate supper with **family**. OK that isn't exactly an attraction, but my guess is just about everyone has family, friends, or old acquaintances somewhere along a great American west road trip. If it's been awhile, look them up and make plans to see them. In our case, this is the first of two sets of people we visited on our vacation.

Since today was a basically just a long travel day, let's take a minute to talk about daylong car rides. We drove 765 miles.

Visit *www.shortandsweetintroductions.com/westlinks* for websites and resources

With stops, it took us about 15 ½ hours to make the drive (but gained an hour with the time change). That's a long time to drive, so here are some tips for days like this:

*Rotate drivers every 1½ to 2 hours. My main exception to this rule is first thing in the morning when most people might be sleeping and everyone can go the longest without stopping to eat or go to the bathroom.

*Make sure everyone goes to the bathroom when you stop. We had six people in our car and it would have been disastrous if one of the kids decided to skip a bathroom stop. No doubt that would mean they would need to stop 45 minutes later.

*Vary your entertainment. Of course, technology makes traveling a little easier, but you might bring along different kinds of entertainment. Aside from videos on our devices, we also brought along old-school DVDs. We even bought a few copies of a book to read together. We never made it through the book, but it did provide a break while driving.

*I bet your car will be packed to the limit, but don't forget to bring a couple of pillows and blankets for traveling. The more people you have in the car, the less likely you will all agree on a comfortable temperature.

*Our least successful meals were ones where we didn't plan them. You may not be a proponent of planning every last detail, but the farther west you drive, the fewer meal options you have. (I'm talking about you Taco Johns in Wyoming!)

*Play games in the car. You can play the license plate game with apps that let you check off states. You can play cows and cemeteries. Use your imagination!

Day 1 Stats

765 miles

Breakfast – home/brought with us

Lunch – Iowa 80 Truck Stop (Walcott, IA)

Supper – Green Mill Restaurant & Bar (Albert Lea, MN) with Minnesota family

Hotel – Clubhouse Hotel & Suites (Sioux Falls, SD) – good place with an indoor pool and waterslide for the kids

Our Route –

> I-74 west out of Indianapolis to the Quad Cities (Illinois and Iowa)
> I-80 west to Iowa City, IA
> I-380 north to Waterloo, IA
> US 218 north to Floyd, IA
> US 18 west to I-35
> I-35 north to I-90
> I-90 west to Sioux Falls, SD

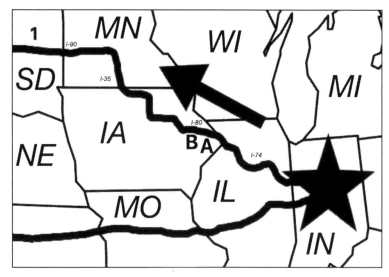

A – Antique Archaeology
B – Iowa 80 Truck Stop
1 – Night 1 in Sioux Falls, SD

Visit *www.shortandsweetintroductions.com/westlinks* for websites and resources

Day 2 – South Dakota (356 miles)

- **Minuteman Missile National Historic Site**
  - **Badlands National Park**
    - **Wall Drug**
    - **Mt. Rushmore**

This is our first real vacation day! Day 1 was basically a lot of driving. Day 2 is when we finally got to start checking things off the list.

Today started with the last part of our driving to make it "out west." We drove about four hours on I-90 from Sioux Falls to exit 131 and the Minuteman Missile National Historic Site. We ate lunch in the visitor center parking lot, and then went into our first official vacation stop.

Minuteman Missile National Historic Site

The Minuteman Missile Visitor Center recounts the Cold War between the United States and Soviet Union by focusing on the hundreds and hundreds of nuclear missiles that were ready in a moment's notice in underground silos across the central United States. The visitor center itself hosts a 30-minute film, an interesting walk-through museum with exhibits, and a gift store.

While we enjoyed the visitor center (which takes about an hour to go through), we didn't make time to visit the two missile silos. Delta-09 is located about 15 minutes away from the visitor center and contains a glass-topped, inground silo with an unarmed missile inside it. You can look down into the silo and learn from an optional, self-guided cell phone tour.

Even cooler than Delta-09 is Delta-01 (about 10 minutes from the visitor center), where you can take a 30-minute tour underground and into the control center of an old missile silo. While the half-hour tours are conducted by a park ranger, they are limited to only six people per tour. To go on the tour, you must have advance reservations (that requires a nominal fee). Same day tours are not available, and because they are limited, the tours fill up very quickly. You may make reservations 90 days in advance and because they fill up quickly, you should plan on making your reservation exactly 90 days before you plan to visit.

Badlands National Park

My parents took my sister and me to Badlands National Park when I was 17. Out of everything we saw on that west trip, Badlands stuck with me as this really cool place that I wanted to see again. As I was taking my family to Badlands on Day 2, I was really excited and also a little nervous that it wouldn't live up to my teenage memories.

But it did! Badlands National Park might be one of the most under-known and totally awesome national parks in the United States. Maybe it's neat partly because you've looked at farms and grasses for a day straight, and maybe partly because it is the first national park of the trip. Regardless, you don't want to miss Badlands National Park.

Have you never heard of it? Words can't do it justice, so stop what you're doing and look at some pictures online (or just look at the cover of this book!).

The best way to describe Badlands National Park is a rocky collection of sharp hills and cliffs, where barely any vegetation grows and you can climb on and around those magnificent, other-worldly hills.

The best way to see Badlands National Park is to take the same I-90 exit as the Minuteman Missile Visitors Center (exit 131) and head south into the park. Then, you can essentially drive on South Dakota Route 240 – Badlands Loop Rd. It is a u-shaped route through the park that takes you back to I-90, 21 miles farther west, at Wall, South Dakota (exit 110).

Most people will alternate driving a few miles with parking and walking around on the rocks. Please be careful, the drops can be steep and people do get seriously injured and even die in this park.

After you first drive into the park (which is located just minutes south of I-90), you will drive for a few minutes and then arrive at the Ben Reifel Visitor Center. The visitor center is a little small, but contains good information about the formation of the Badlands, the animals that live there, and the fossils that people still discover there.

As you continue driving Badlands Loop Rd., you might decide to play on the rocks or hike on a trail. Be sure to get information about each trail in the visitor center and understand their lengths and difficulty levels (including how much vertical hiking you will have to do for each one).

Seeing wildlife will be a highlight of your visit. You might see bison on the surrounding prairie, bighorn sheep climbing on the rocks, pronghorn (not antelope), and adorable prairie dogs. It's also worth mentioning that you should be on the lookout for snakes when you walk on the rocks.

While stops along Badlands Loop Rd. might be enough for you, there are some additional side routes that take you to less-visited parts of the park. Badlands National Park extends pretty far west and south of Badlands Loop Rd. Badlands National Park contains a lodge and two campgrounds, as well as unlimited opportunities for backcountry camping.

It's also worth noting that Badlands National Park is well-known for its nighttime star gazing. Unfortunately, we weren't there at dark, though I really want to go back at night some time.

Like other national parks, you have to pay to enter Badlands National Park.

Wall Drug

It seems kind of weird to talk about one of America's best national parks and then a drug store back to back, but it's nearly impossible to visit South Dakota on I-90 and not stop by Wall Drug. Wall Drug is located in Wall, SD, just off I-90 at exit 110, and is at the end of the western part of Badlands Loop Rd.

Originally a small drug store, Wall Drug began offering free cold water to motorists on their way to visit Mount Rushmore. Through billboard advertising literally around the world, Wall Drug quickly grew into a huge tourist trap, complete with thousands of square feet of shops, restaurants, artwork, and attractions. Many people stop for a meal, some souvenirs, and of course, free water.

Mount Rushmore

On our trip, we visited the Minuteman Missile Visitors Center, drove through Badlands National Park, stopped by Wall Drug, and then headed west a little less than an hour to Rapid City. While there we ate supper, checked into our hotel, and then drove about a half hour to Mount Rushmore.

The first thing you need to know is that Mount Rushmore is in Black Hills National Forest. There is so much more to the Black Hills than Mount Rushmore – I'll include some of those things in the honorable mention after this section of the book.

You will wind your way up mountains to get to Mount Rushmore. The roads are nice and are made to accommodate the thousands of daily visitors to Mount Rushmore. Once you are there, you don't have to pay an admission fee, but you will pay a parking fee. Most people take one to two hours and visit the Lincoln Borglum Visitor Center (movies, exhibits, and viewing seats), take a walk around the Presidential Trail (which offers a closer and unique look at Mount Rushmore), and visit the Sculptor's Studio. If you have more time, you might attend a ranger talk or eat in the restaurant.

We visited Mount Rushmore in the late evening, so we were able to watch the Evening Lighting Ceremony. During this ceremony, a ranger talks about the monument and then it lights up. It's pretty to see it lit up at night, but we learned the hard way that you need to be seated in the amphitheater to hear the ranger speaking.

Day 2 Stats

356 miles

Breakfast – at our hotel

Lunch – picnic lunch we brought with us to the Minuteman Missile visitor center

Supper – Texas Roadhouse (Rapid City, SD)

Hotel – Lazy U Motel (Rapid City, SD) – it had good reviews, but is a basic, small roadside hotel

Our Route –

> I-90 west to exit 131
> Cottonwood Rd. north to Minuteman Missile Visitor Center
> Cottonwood Rd./ South Dakota Route 240 south (becomes Badlands Loop Rd.) and looping through Badlands back to I-90 in Wall, SD (with a brief excursion down Sagecreek Rim Rd.)
> I-90 west to Rapid City, SD
> US 16 west into the Black Hills
> US 16A to Mount Rushmore
> US 16A back to US 16, then back to Rapid City, SD

A Short and Sweet Introduction to the Great American West Vacation

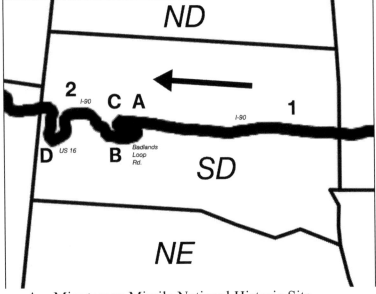

A – Minuteman Missile National Historic Site
B – Badlands National Park
C – Wall Drug
D – Mt. Rushmore
1 – Night 1 in Sioux Falls, SD
2 – Night 2 in Rapid City, SD

Visit *www.shortandsweetintroductions.com/westlinks* for websites and resources

Honorable Mention – Black Hills National Forest

- Wind Cave National Park
  - Custer State Park
  - Crazy Horse Memorial
- Jewel Cave National Monument
  - Other Black Hills Attractions

The Black Hills is a mountain range that rises out of the Great Plains and is separate from the Rocky Mountains farther west. Located in western South Dakota and eastern Wyoming, the Black Hills climb in elevation to over 7,000 feet, which is taller than any mountain in the entire eastern United States. The Black Hills are absolutely beautiful and contain animals such as mule deer, elk, bighorn sheep, mountain lions, and pronghorn. A variety of roads crisscross the Black Hills, containing towns, natural attractions and man-made attractions.

On our trip, we visited Mount Rushmore on Day 2, as well as Sturgis and Deadwood on Day 3, so I won't talk about those places in this honorable mention, though they would certainly be a part of any trip to the Black Hills.

Wind Cave National Park

Wind Cave National Park sits in the southeast corner of the Black Hills (about one hour south of Rapid City). The cave system is the sixth-longest known cave system in the world and is known for its boxwork, a unique cave wall feature. Wind Cave is named for the winds found at its entrance and it also contains the largest natural prairie grassland above it.

Wind Cave National Park is served by a year-round visitor center and is a national park that doesn't charge an admission fee. However, you do have to pay a fee to tour the cave. If you visit, please note that the visitor center is located on Highway 385 – some GPS units incorrectly place the visitor center on Highway 87.

With the exception of a campground, there are no services in the park (including restaurants). Aside from visiting the cave, you can hike the park's trails, camp in the backcountry (in a designated area only), and view wildlife, including bison, elk, pronghorn, and prairie dogs. It is worth noting that the Wind Cave bison herd (250-400 animals) is one of only a small number of known free-roaming, genetically pure bison herds in the United States.

Custer State Park

Custer State Park is a South Dakota state park located directly north of Wind Cave National Park and south of Mount Rushmore. Custer State Park is a large, preserved area of the Black Hills. Famous for its wildlife viewing, Wildlife Loop Rd. is a popular drive through the park.

While in the park, you can camp, hike, bike, swim, cross-country ski, fish, canoe, kayak, paddleboard, and more. The park is famous for its yearly buffalo roundup, where the park's over 1,000 buffalo are rounded up and then a portion of them sold through auction to keep the park's population at a manageable level. Also unique is the park's "begging burros," a population of donkeys that roam the park and beg visitors for free food!

Custer State Park is home to a variety of lodges, campsites, and restaurants. There is an admission fee to the park.

Visit *www.shortandsweetintroductions.com/westlinks* for websites and resources

Crazy Horse Memorial

Located about 25 minutes west of Mount Rushmore, Crazy Horse Memorial is another mountain sculpture and honors Crazy Horse, a leader of the Oglala Lakota tribe in the 1800s. Crazy Horse earned fame by leading Native Americans against Custer in the Battle of the Little Bighorn.

Crazy Horse Memorial is a work in progress. It is not operated by the U.S. government, but rather by the Crazy Horse Memorial Foundation. As such, it has an admission fee (with options per person or per carload), and admission is not covered by any U.S. National Parks passes.

In addition to viewing the memorial, there is a visitor center that tells the story of Crazy Horse and contains Native American art and artifacts. The visitor center has a restaurant, conference facilities, and gift shop.

Jewel Cave National Monument

Located about 45 minutes west of Mt. Rushmore, Jewel Cave National Monument is the third-longest mapped cave system in the world (Kentucky's Mammoth Cave is first). Open year-round, visitors can take one of three tours in the cave, as well as hike on trails above ground.

Jewel Cave National Monument is served by a visitor center with restrooms but does not contain a restaurant. Two of the three cave tours originate from the visitor center area, while the third tour originates about a mile west (where there is a parking lot and restrooms).

Tours require a paid ticket. You can reserve tickets in advance or purchase them day-of. As of this book's publishing, only one of the tours is free through various national parks and monuments passes.

Another notable feature of Jewel Cave National Monument is that almost 90% of its trees burned in a fire in 2000. What remains is the regrowth of the forest, a neat study in how a forest recovers from a fire.

Other Black Hills Attractions

While the Black Hills offers a wide variety of parks and monuments, there are also a variety of manmade attractions. You can ride a steam train, navigate a ropes course, ride a mountain rollercoaster, tour a mystery house, ride a zipline, visit animal exhibits, tour gold mines, and more. Furthermore, there are various hotels, lodges, cabins, ranches, and resorts throughout the Black Hills.

Visit *www.shortandsweetintroductions.com/westlinks* for websites and resources

Day 3 – South Dakota, Wyoming, and Montana (527 miles)

- Sturgis
- Deadwood
- Devil's Tower
- Little Bighorn Battlefield

On this day we finished our brief tour of the Black Hills area and hit a couple of sights on our way to Yellowstone National Park. This day's drive is highlighted by views of the Rocky Mountains as we approached the front range and then as we went north around it.

On our trip today was July 4th. Even though we were driving through rural Montana after dark, we still saw glimpses of fireworks from towns around I-90.

Please understand that this day's route isn't the most direct route to Yellowstone National Park. We chose this route to see Little Bighorn Battlefield, which means we started our Yellowstone tour (Days 4 and 5) from Yellowstone's North Entrance. If either you don't want to see Little Bighorn, you aren't traveling farther north to Glacier National Park, or you don't care to go through the North Entrance (and the Roosevelt Arch), then your quickest route to Yellowstone is west through Cody, Wyoming (which is also a popular tourist spot). You can actually start your Yellowstone tour from any of its five entrances.

Sturgis

This was just a picture stop for us, but Sturgis is THE destination for thousands of bikers. Host of a wildly popular (and just plain wild) annual motorcycle rally, Sturgis is a small town on the edge of the Black Hills.

We simply drove through town and took some pictures, but people are drawn to various bars and restaurants, as well as the Sturgis Motorcycle Museum & Hall of Fame. We didn't have a motorcycle, just a minivan. We felt a little out of place!

Deadwood

A successful (and commercial) preservation of a classic western gold rush town, Deadwood, South Dakota is the site of the death of Wild Bill Hickok. Today Deadwood hosts a variety of restaurants, casinos, shops, and hotels on its classic Main St. Deadwood is also the setting for the former HBO series of the same name.

More than just gambling and eating, Deadwood has become a resort destination with nice amenities. Deadwood hosts concerts and festivals throughout the year, gun fight reenactments along Main St., as well as tours of the town and surrounding areas.

While it is in the Black Hills, Deadwood is over an hour's drive north of most of the parks and monuments. Regardless, many people make Deadwood their vacation hub because of the restaurants and entertainment, while making day trips out of Deadwood for the other Black Hills attractions.

Devil's Tower

After leaving Deadwood, we drove a couple of hours into Wyoming to Devil's Tower. A U.S. monument, Devil's Tower is a cylindrical rock tower that extends over 1,000 feet straight up from the land around it. Popular because of its unusual appearance, Devil's Tower offers hiking around the base of the tower and rock climbing straight up the tower. Devil's Tower was highlighted in Steven Spielberg's movie, *Close Encounters of the Third Kind.*

As the tower is the primary attraction, nearly all visitors park at the visitor center where there are restrooms and information about Devil's Tower. There is not a restaurant or lodge, though you can camp (no hookups available). Like other national parks and monuments, there is an admission fee (based per vehicle).

Climbing Devil's Tower is on many rock climbers' bucket lists. To climb it, you are required to get a free permit. There are various climbing routes of various difficulty. It is also worth noting that there is a voluntary climbing closure in June out of respect for the cultural and spiritual value some Native American tribes ascribe to Devil's Tower.

Perhaps one of the highlights of a trip to Devil's Tower is a prairie dog colony located along the main park road, just after you enter the park. You can pull off the road and see dozens of prairie dogs peeking up above the ground and racing across the prairie.

Please note that Devil's Tower is a little off the beaten path. The roads (two-lane) to get to the park are easy to drive, but it isn't necessarily a quick stop off of your route from Black Hills to Yellowstone. Expect to add a total of 45-60 minutes of driving to your day to go to and from Devil's Tower.

Little Bighorn Battlefield

After Devil's Tower we drove farther west and then north into Montana to Little Bighorn Battlefield. Just a couple of weeks before the United States' 100th birthday in 1876, George Custer led 700 men to battle against 2,500 of Crazy Horse's Native Americans. Custer's men were badly defeated, and the victory was among the last major victories for Native Americans in the United States.

The Little Bighorn Battlefield is conveniently located just off I-90 in southeastern Montana, directly on your route from Devil's Tower to hotels in Livingston, MT. Comprised of two separate battlefields, you can visit the visitor center (restrooms, but no restaurant) and then take a self-guided walking/driving tour of Custer National Cemetery, battlefields, and monuments for both Custer's men and Native American men.

Please note that you don't have to spend a lot of time at Little Bighorn Battlefield, but it doesn't stay open particularly late (especially in the fall, winter, and spring).

Day 3 Stats

527 miles

Breakfast – fast food (Rapid City, SD)

Lunch – picnic lunch we brought with us to Devil's Tower

Supper – fast food – Taco John's – not a great experience (Sheridan, WY)

Hotel – Livingston Inn (Livingston, MT) – one of the weirdest rooms I've ever had! Our room seemed to be the owner's former apartment. It was located in the basement, past the washer and dryer. It was big and a little creepy.

Our Route –

> I-90 west to exit 32, Sturgis
> We drove around Sturgis a little
> Alt US 14 west from Sturgis to Deadwood
> US 85 north from Deadwood to I-90
> I-90 west to exit 185 in Wyoming
> US 14 west to Wyoming Route 24
> Wyoming Route 24 north to Devil's Tower, then back to US 14
> US 14 west to I-90 (don't go back the way you came on US 14)

Visit *www.shortandsweetintroductions.com/westlinks* for websites and resources

I-90 west to Livingston, MT (with a stop at exit 510 in Montana for Little Bighorn)

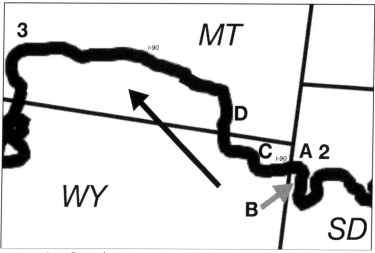

A – Sturgis
B – Deadwood
C – Devil's Tower
D – Little Bighorn Battlefield
2 – Night 2 in Rapid City, SD
3 – Night 3 in Livingston, MT

A Short and Sweet Introduction to the Great American West Vacation

Honorable Mention – Glacier National Park

It seems a little silly to give such a grand park an honorable mention, but we just didn't have time for it on our trip. Located about 5½ hours north of where we stayed in Livingston, MT, Glacier National Park is home to 25 glaciers and a large number of mountain peaks, lakes, and animals.

One of the highlights of the park is Going-to-the-Sun Rd., the only road that traverses through the park east and west. Due to the park's far-northern location and high elevation, the road is often not completely open because of snow until June, and then closes again around October. If you travel to the park outside of this window, you can still drive the road as far as it is plowed open.

Glacier National park is served by three visitor centers, seven lodges and hotels, 13 campgrounds, and several picnic areas and trails. Each lodge area has dining options. Please note, there are no gas stations anywhere in the park.

Shortly after Going-to-the-Sun Rd. opens in the summer, Glacier National Park offers a unique, free shuttle system that takes you from the east entrance (St. Mary Visitor Center) and the west entrance (Apgar Visitor Center) to the mountaintop Logan Pass Visitor Center. The shuttle provides a stress-free way to enjoy the view, take some pictures, and reduce vehicular pollution in the park.

There are a variety of tour companies that offer paid tours. You can also stay in a variety of hotels and cabins outside of the park.

Like other national parks, there is an entrance fee.

Visit *www.shortandsweetintroductions.com/westlinks* for websites and resources

Day 4 – Yellowstone National Park (1st Day) (163 miles)

- North Entrance
- Mammoth Hot Springs
- Undine Falls, Blacktail Plateau Drive, Petrified Tree
- Roosevelt Lodge and Lamar Valley
- Tower Fall
- Canyon Village
- Upper and Lower Falls
- Artist Paintpots
- Boiling River

Wow! This list looks overwhelming! I remember being exhausted at the end of this day, and looking back, it's easy to see why. This was a 12-hour day for us (even though we planned for 13 hours!). The most significant driving was the one-hour trip from Livingston to the North Entrance. After that, our day was a constant repetition of drive, stop to look and walk, then repeat.

On this day, we saw bison, moose, bear, and elk. We saw waterfalls and mountains. We saw unique thermal features and just really soaked in being in one of the most beautiful places in the world.

A few notes about Yellowstone before we get into the next two days:

1) Please know that it is very dangerous to walk off of the paths or wooden walkways near any thermal features. People die every year when they don't heed this basic warning.

2) Yellowstone is very popular and just about every major attraction is on Grand Loop Rd, which makes a large oval around the park. There is a second major road (Norris Canyon Rd.) that cuts across the middle, creating a large figure 8. That makes planning to visit Yellowstone pretty easy (we visited the top loop on Day 4 and the bottom loop on Day 5). That being said, these roads carry a lot of traffic, especially in the summer. And, if there are any neat animals near the road, then traffic will stop and might become impassible.

3) There are eight different visitor centers and museums. Don't think that once you've seen one, you've seen them all. Each visitor center focuses on different aspects of the park.

4) The animals might seem tame, but they're not! True, many of the animals are used to seeing people and might have more tolerance for you getting close to them than animals in other places. However, people are seriously injured and killed by animals at Yellowstone and it's often due to poor decisions by the humans, not the animals. When there are potentially dangerous animals in the area (bears, male elk, etc.), park employees and volunteers usually help manage traffic and keep people safe.

5) Yellowstone is spectacular in that so many of its cool features are right beside Grand Loop Rd. That makes for several spots of quick pull-offs and an opportunity to walk around and take pictures without having to hike through the park. In fact, much of the park is accessible by people who use wheelchairs and other devices.

6) It doesn't get very hot in Yellowstone. In fact, it's not impossible to see snow flurries in the summer! Most summer

days are pleasant but might require a jacket or sweatshirt. Evenings can get chilly, so plan accordingly.

7) There are several more things to see in Yellowstone than I am listing here. At some point we had to prioritize the sights and try to see examples of each type of feature.

8) There are an abundance of lodging and camping options inside the park. However, Yellowstone is so popular that many options fill up months in advance.

North Entrance

Our drive started about an hour north in Livingston, MT. The drive south into Yellowstone is essentially an hour-long drive through a long valley with mountains rising on both sides. Right before you get into Yellowstone, you pass through Gardiner, MT, a small town with hotels and restaurants (where we came back to spend this night). The North Entrance is marked by the Roosevelt Arch, a large brick arch entryway whose cornerstone was laid by President Teddy Roosevelt. The North Entrance is the only Yellowstone entrance that is open year-round to cars because it is the only way to access Cooke City, MT, on the northeast side of the park in the winter. You pay your entrance fee to get into Yellowstone at the North Entrance (or any of its five entrances).

Mammoth Hot Springs

Mammoth Hot Springs is about five miles into Yellowstone from the North Entrance and is where the U.S. Army and then the National Park Service first managed Yellowstone. There are many buildings in this area, including the Albright Visitor Center, which is worth a stop for an orientation to the park. From here you choose to go east or south, beginning your trek on Grand Loop Rd. On the day that we were there, there were several elk lying in the grass by the buildings, like pet dogs. Remember, keep your distance!

The hot springs were our first natural attraction in Yellowstone and it is probably different from anything else you've ever seen. The hot springs are a succession of extremely hot water seeping out of the ground and running down the hill. The entire area is covered in minerals and looks other-worldly. There are a variety of walkways you can use to explore the large area. If you choose, drive Upper Terrace Loop Dr. for a more extensive look at the area.

Undine Falls, Blacktail Plateau Drive, Petrified Tree

As we set off east across the north part of Grand Loop Rd., our first stop was for a quick picture of Undine Falls. Next, instead of remaining on Grand Loop Rd., we took the one-way route Blacktail Plateau Drive, which winds a little off the beaten path before rejoining Grand Loop Rd. We took it in hopes of seeing animals but didn't have any luck. Just past where we rejoined Grand Loop Rd., we took a short detour to view a petrified tree.

Roosevelt Lodge and Lamar Valley

Completing our trip across the north part of Grand Loop Rd., we made a pit stop at Roosevelt Lodge. From there we decided to head off Grand Loop Rd. again and go a few miles down Northeast Entrance Rd. to eat lunch at a picnic area and then to go to Lamar Valley, the home of one of Yellowstone's bison herds. While picnicking, we watched a family of black bears descend the mountain across from us. After our picnic we got some neat pictures of the bison herd before turning around and heading back to Grand Loop Rd.

Tower Fall

Next, we started our route south on the eastern leg of Grand Loop Rd. On the way we stopped by Tower Fall and took some pictures. This was an especially busy and crazy stop. It was hard to find a parking spot and the place is so popular that there is a general store at the stop. As you drive this section of Grand Loop Rd., you can see the scenic Yellowstone River at times to the east and you also drive through Dunraven Pass, the highest elevation you will drive through in Yellowstone (almost 8,900 feet).

Canyon Village

Canyon Village is at the junction of Grand Loop Rd. and Norris Canyon Rd. (the road that cuts across the middle of Yellowstone). We visited the Canyon Village Visitor Center and saw a neat, large 3-D map of the entire park. Nearby we saw two bison very close to the road – much closer than the herd we saw in Lamar Valley.

Upper and Lower Falls

Although this day's plan had us driving west across Norris Canyon Rd. and keeping the park divided into two loops, we did continue a little south of Canyon Village to see the Upper and Lower Falls. We could have spent more time here – there are a few trails, but we didn't have time. However, it is worth your time to keep driving past Upper Falls to see Lower Falls. When you are there, you can look north past Lower Falls as the water flows downstream and see the scenic Grand Canyon of the Yellowstone. It was while driving between the two falls that we had our neatest animal encounter – a very large male elk crossed the road right in front of our car. It made for a really cool video.

Artist Paintpots

After driving west across Norris Canyon Rd. to rejoin the west side of Grand Loop Rd., we had intended on visiting Porcelain Basin Trail, Back Basin Loop, Gibbon Falls, and Artist Paintpots. We decided we had to draw the line somewhere (we were tired), so we just visited Artist Paintpots. This was our longest "hike" of Yellowstone – a one-mile trail through the woods that took us to Artist Paintpots, a collection of mud pots, hot springs, and geysers. I'm glad we did it, but it really made us tired.

Boiling River

After Artist Paint Pot we headed north on Grand Loop Rd. back to Mammoth Hot Springs. From there we traveled the five miles back to Gardiner, MT. Although we were exhausted, I really wanted to stop by Boiling River (on the road back to Gardiner). Here we parked and then walked a path to a place where a hot spring pours into the Gardiner River, creating a swirl of hot and cold waters to swim and play in. Our kids got pretty wet and I just dipped in my feet. It is a popular spot.

Day 4 Stats

163 miles

Breakfast – fast food and items from a local grocery store

Lunch – picnic near Roosevelt Lodge

Supper – local restaurant (Gardiner, MT) – it was kind of late; we probably would have had more energy had we eaten earlier

Hotel – Super 8 (Gardiner, MT) – while we were driving to our hotel that night, we saw a female elk walking down the center of town

Our Route –

    US 89 south into Yellowstone
    Grand Loop Rd. east to Tower Junction (with a detour on the one-way Blacktail Plateau Dr.)
    A short drive out NE Entrance Rd. and then back to Grand Loop Rd.
    Grand Loop Rd. south to Canyon Village
    Briefly south on Grand Loop Rd. to S Rim Dr. (Upper and Lower Falls), then back to Grand Loop Rd. and Canyon Village

Visit *www.shortandsweetintroductions.com/westlinks* for websites and resources

West on Norris Canyon Rd. to the other side of Yellowstone

A short trip south on Grand Loop Rd. to Artist Paintpots

North on Grand Loop Rd. (this section is US 89) back to Mammoth

Continue on US 89 to Gardiner, MT

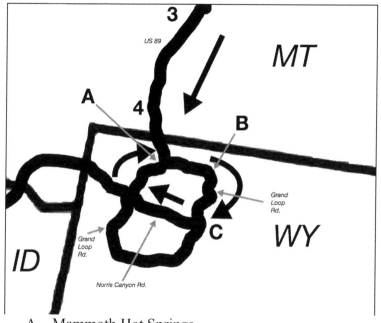

A – Mammoth Hot Springs
B – Roosevelt Lodge
C – Canyon Village
3 – Night 3 in Livingston, MT
4 – Night 4 in Gardiner, MT

Day 5 – Yellowstone National Park (2nd Day) (269 miles)

- Sulphur Caldron, Mud Volcano, Dragon's Mouth Spring
  - Yellowstone Lake
    - Old Faithful
  - Grand Prismatic Spring
  - The Drive in Idaho

I'm going to admit that we were a little tired by this day and knew that we had a 2+ hour drive once we left Yellowstone that evening. I think the combination of the long day on the previous day and the idea that everything in Yellowstone is so unique and interesting, that it all kind of became the same and wore us out.

I don't know that I would do it differently, especially since the purpose of this vacation was to see so much in 14 days. But, I wouldn't rule out a future trip to Yellowstone that spreads out the sights over more days and allows for a little more rest and reflection while in the park.

That being said, our day started from Gardiner, MT, which meant we had about an hour and a half of driving over roads that we had already driven to get us to the east side of Grand Loop Rd. at Canyon Village. Once there, we started the new part of our trip by heading south down the lower loop of Grand Loop Rd. As we first headed south past Canyon Village, we drove through Hayden Valley, a popular wildlife viewing spot. We didn't see anything though.

Visit *www.shortandsweetintroductions.com/westlinks* for websites and resources

Sulphur Caldron, Mud Volcano, Dragon's Mouth Spring

These three sights are literally across the road from each other and feature bubbling, smelly pots of goop coming out of the ground. Sulphur Caldron is right beside the road and you pretty much look at it where you park your car. Mud Volcano and Dragon's Mouth Spring are also right beside the road but have wooden walkways that you can use to get closer.

Yellowstone Lake

This is the biggest lake in the United States above 7,000 feet. At some points Grand Loop Rd. is right beside the lake. We stopped and had lunch at Lake Lodge, which provided a good view of the lake. There's also a visitor center at the lake (Fishing Bridge Visitor Center) that we didn't stop at.

You can camp and lodge at Yellowstone Lake as well as boat on your own boat or a rented boat. In fact, some trails on the south part of Yellowstone Lake are more quickly accessed by boating to them.

West Thumb Geyser Basin is located on the west part of Yellowstone Lake. We parked here to have a look, but when we arrived we saw on a message board that Old Faithful was erupting relatively soon. We really wanted to catch this next eruption so that we didn't have to wait another hour and a half, so we left West Thumb Geyser Basin without looking around. Had we stayed at West Thumb Geyser Basin, we could have seen small geysers and very hot pools of water.

Old Faithful

This is the main attraction at Yellowstone National Park. Often erupting over 100 feet into the air about every 1½ hours, Old Faithful can attract thousands of people per eruption. It is a very built-up area of Yellowstone, containing three park hotels, a visitor center, a U.S. post office, and restaurants.

Benches flank the south side of Old Faithful, though you'll have to get there early to get a seat. Many people have to stand to watch the eruption, but it certainly goes high enough for everyone to see.

Old Faithful is part of a larger geyser basin that has a variety of geysers – varied in size and eruptions. We actually saw another geyser erupt in the distance while standing at Old Faithful. You can hike trails in the area to get closer to the other geysers.

A couple of facts I learned from a ranger talk:

*Half of all the geysers in the world are in this particular geyser basin.

*2,000-3,000 earthquakes occur here every year, though you won't likely feel them.

*In 1969, a large earthquake caused 169 geysers to erupt – 60 that had never erupted before and one that erupted for 100 straight hours.

Grand Prismatic Spring

Grand Prismatic Spring is a beautiful, photogenic, colorful hot spring. That is, if you can see it. On the day we visited, the wind swirled the steam from the spring and surrounding hot pools, so we couldn't see the Grand Prismatic Spring very well.

The only way to see the spring is to walk on an elevated wood boardwalk around the pools and up to the spring. I'll admit, it's a little scary. The wind was pretty strong on the day we visited and I worried a little about what would happen if I fell off the boardwalk. More dangerous parts of the boardwalk have railings, but all of it doesn't.

It is worth reminding you that people die every year at Yellowstone when they venture off of the marked trails and boardwalks or they try to touch hot water.

Visit *www.shortandsweetintroductions.com/westlinks* for websites and resources

The Drive in Idaho

After we left Yellowstone through West Yellowstone, Montana, we drove a bit over 2 hours to our hotel. There are two things you might notice while driving through Idaho. First, the large mountain range to the east is the Grand Tetons. It is pretty magnificent and you can read about it in the next "Honorable Mention." Second, as you drive south on Interstate 15, you go through a unique place called Hell's Half Acre Lava Field. The 150 square mile area is the remnants of an old lava flow. It is pretty neat to see and you can view it as you drive on the interstate. I didn't know it then, but both the northbound and southbound rest areas in the lava field contain short trails that you can take to hike through the field when you park at the rest areas.

Day 5 Stats

269 miles

Breakfast – hotel

Lunch – Lake Lodge at Yellowstone Lake

Supper – local restaurant (West Yellowstone, MT)

Hotel – Shoshone-Bannock Hotel and Convention Center (Fort Hall, ID) – this is a hotel located on the Fort Hall Indian Reservation just off Interstate 15. It was a nice and affordable hotel. Our shower was even an all-tile, walk in shower.

Our Route –

   US 89 south into Yellowstone
   Grand Loop Rd. south to Norris Canyon Rd.
   Norris Canyon Rd. east to Canyon Village
   Grand Loop Rd. south, then west (it joins with US
     20), and then north (it joins with US 191)
   Continue on US 20/191 west out of Yellowstone

US 20 west from West Yellowstone, MT to I-15 in Idaho
I-15 south to Fort Hall, ID

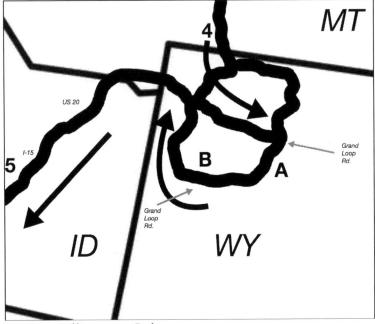

A – Yellowstone Lake
B – Old Faithful
4 – Night 4 in Gardiner, MT
5 – Night 5 in Fort Hall, ID

Visit *www.shortandsweetintroductions.com/westlinks* for websites and resources

Honorable Mention – Grand Tetons, Salt Lake City and Zion National Park

- Grand Teton National Park and Jackson Hole
  - Salt Lake City
  - Zion National Park

When we first planned our trip, we never even thought of driving to San Francisco. While we planned to go to Los Angeles, we were going to drive there roundtrip from Las Vegas. So, our trip would have taken us south from Yellowstone to the Grand Tetons, then through Salt Lake City, by Zion National Park, and on to Las Vegas. You might choose this route instead, so here is a brief overview.

Grand Teton National Park and Jackson Hole

Grand Teton National Park is less than an hour's drive south of Grand Loop Rd. in Yellowstone. Grand Teton National Park's focus is the Teton Mountain range, a majestic set of summits which sharply rise on the west side of the park. It is possible to appreciate the park simply by driving through it and enjoying the view, though there are a number of visitor centers, cabins, lodges, and restaurants in the park.

Jackson Hole is the name of the area south of Grand Teton National Park. It is named "hole" because it sits in a large valley with mountains on nearly every side. Jackson, WY, is the primary town in the region and is noted for its tourism, ski resorts, and mountain homes of the rich and famous.

Salt Lake City

Located about five hours south and slightly west of Grand Teton National Park, Salt Lake City is the capital of Utah. Nestled against the mountains, Salt Lake City is well-known as the headquarters for the Mormon Church. Nearby is Great Salt Lake, whose salinity is so high, you can float on the water. Also nearby is Park City, a well-known ski resort.

Zion National Park

Renowned for its mountainous desert beauty, Zion National Park is about 4½ hours south of Salt Lake City and 2½ hours northeast of Las Vegas. Hiking is popular in the park, though keep in mind that it can get very hot – you must bring water. Zion National Park is located relatively close to Interstate 15, but you will have to plan a total drive of 1½ hours roundtrip to get to the park and then back to the interstate.

Visit *www.shortandsweetintroductions.com/westlinks* for websites and resources

Day 6 – Driving with a Stop by Lake Tahoe (809 miles)

- Lake Tahoe

When we started Day 6, I was really looking forward to an off-day. The idea of highway driving for the whole day actually sounded relaxing compared to the mountain roads and stop-and-go of Yellowstone National Park. By the end of the day, however, I was totally over it and vowed I would never again drive through northern Nevada!

Our trip started with about two hours of interstate in Idaho. Our route generally followed the Snake River. When you get off the interstate in Twin Falls, ID, the Snake River Canyon is an unexpected and pleasant view as you cross the Snake River.

After leaving Twin Falls, we drove a two-lane road south into Nevada (it is called the Great Basin Highway in Nevada). Driving the road was fine – it is really straight and easy to pass cars if you ever encounter any. Don't plan on getting gas while you're on this stretch of road! Along the route are some neat wildlife bridge crossings that Nevada has constructed to help save human lives and animal lives during animal migrations.

After connecting with Interstate 80 in Nevada, we essentially took that all the way to San Francisco. The Nevada part was crazy boring and didn't have much to look at. We were excited to see civilization at Reno and we also made a detour off I-80 to see Lake Tahoe before rejoining I-80 in California.

Lake Tahoe

Lake Tahoe holds a few distinctions – the largest alpine lake (5,000 feet above sea level) in the United States, the largest U.S. lake by volume after the five Great Lakes, and the second deepest lake in the United States.

Lake Tahoe sits on the Nevada-California border with ski resorts in the surrounding mountains and cabins, hotels, restaurants, and tourist attractions around the lake.

When traveling from the east through Nevada, ascending the mountains into Lake Tahoe (with all of the trees and vegetation) is a welcome change. While Reno sits in the desert just miles from Lake Tahoe, Lake Tahoe can receive over 100 inches of snow in a year and the surrounding mountains can receive hundreds more! Our first glimpses of Lake Tahoe were beautiful – it was definitely worth the detour off I-80.

For our trip, we just wanted to see Lake Tahoe, so we drove Route 431 from Reno to Lake Tahoe, drove a few miles beside the lake, and then took Route 267 from Lake Tahoe back to I-80 in California.

If you follow our trip, I would **strongly suggest** that you find supper at Lake Tahoe. We made the mistake of planning to eat when we reconnected with I-80 in California. I think half of us ate something from a grocery store and the others ate something gross and forgettable from a local fast food restaurant.

Day 6 Stats

809 miles (second most driving day)

Breakfast – hotel

Lunch – truck stop (Wells, NV)

Supper – grocery store, forgotten fast food (Truckee, CA)

Hotel – Hyatt Place (Dublin, CA) – we chose to stay outside of San Francisco near a BART station. This is the first hotel that we stayed at for multiple nights. That was a nice change from the single stays of our first five nights!

Our Route –

> I-15 south to I-86
> I-86 west to I-84
> I-84 west to exit 173 (Twin Falls, ID)
> US 93 south to I-80 in Wells, NV
> I-80 west to I-580 in Reno, NV
> I-580 south to Nevada route 431
> Nevada 431 south to Tahoe Blvd at Nevada Route 28
> Nevada 28 west to California Route 267
> California 267 north to I-80
> I-80 west to San Francisco

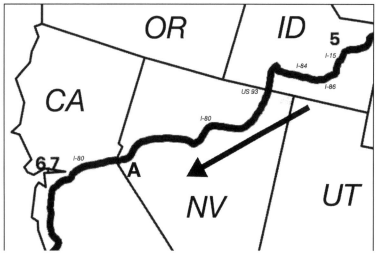

A – Lake Tahoe
5 – Night 5 in Fort Hall, ID
6,7 – Nights 6 and 7 in Dublin, CA

Day 7 – San Francisco (0 miles)

- Alcatraz
- Fisherman's Wharf
- Bus tour
- Golden Gate Bridge

No driving!!! We planned this day so that we didn't have to drive into San Francisco. We took a BART (Bay Area Rapid Transit) train instead of driving. I'm not sure it saved us a lot of time, but it was nice to not be in our van!

The BART train took us into downtown. There are some local streetcars that go from downtown to Fisherman's Wharf, which is the area where many of the attractions are. We were on a schedule and not too sure about the streetcars, so we walked about one mile to the Alcatraz boat launch in Fisherman's Wharf from downtown San Francisco.

Alcatraz

For a place that only operated as a federal prison for less than 30 years, Alcatraz certainly captures our imagination. Set on an island in the bay, Alcatraz Island contains a handful of buildings, with the main building being the prison.

We really enjoyed Alcatraz. You take a boat over to Alcatraz where you can watch a film and tour the island on your own. The highlight of the island is the recorded tour that you take of the prison. With several languages available, you borrow a clean set of headphones and a digital player that directs you and teaches you as you walk through the prison. I've never used a recording as a tour guide, but it was really worth it.

Visit *www.shortandsweetintroductions.com/westlinks* for websites and resources

You also get some neat views of San Francisco while taking the ferry to and from Alcatraz Island.

Alcatraz Cruises is the only ferry boat operator to take you to the island. Your ticket gives you both admission to the island (including the audio tour) and a roundtrip ride on the ferry. You can purchase tickets in advance, which is strongly encouraged. Tickets are timed, so you need to plan your day around your reserved time.

Fisherman's Wharf

This area stretches along the bay and is the tourist destination of San Francisco. There are blocks and blocks of shops, restaurants, and attractions. You can interact with science at the Exploratorium, view animals in the Aquarium of the Bay, climb aboard the World War II USS Pampanito, visit Ghirardelli Square, take tours, and much more! There's even a Ripley's Believe It or Not and Madame Tussauds wax museum.

Bus Tour

I think that bus tours are a great way to see and learn about places in a short amount of time. We took a great bus tour in Washington DC and a mediocre one in New York City. This tour, however, was neither great nor mediocre – it was terrible!

Let's just say, sometimes you get what you pay for and it pays to read reviews. We had good luck with Groupon purchases later in the trip in Los Angeles, but the Groupon purchase we made for our San Francisco bus tour was bad.

Our tour guide did a "good job" of reading road signs aloud to us, incorrectly identifying buildings, and driving in a way that made a pedestrian throw his drink at our bus window. I really believe that a bus tour should be a good way to see San

Francisco (after all, it is an easy way to get to the Golden Gate Bridge), but please, please, please read the reviews!

Golden Gate Bridge

When they say San Francisco is foggy, they aren't kidding. In fact, during the summer, the fog is particularly bad and the weather isn't that warm. We were actually pretty cold on this day – we weren't really prepared for that. The climate in San Francisco is usually colder in the middle of the summer versus the early fall.

So, because of the fog we had obstructed views of the Golden Gate Bridge throughout the day. Later in the day when we took our tour bus to the bridge, the fog briefly let up before quickly enveloping it again. Visiting the bridge is definitely a bucket list item, but you probably won't spend much time there unless you choose to walk across it. You can get some good pictures but beware of the fog!

Day 7 Stats

0 miles

Breakfast – hotel

Lunch – various places in Fisherman's Wharf

Supper – various places in Fisherman's Wharf

Hotel – Hyatt Place (Dublin, CA)

Our Route –

    Dublin/Pleasanton BART station to/from San Francisco

Visit *www.shortandsweetintroductions.com/westlinks* for websites and resources

Day 8 – Pacific Coast (386 miles)

- Henry Cowell Redwoods State Park
  - Carmel Mission
  - Pacific Coast Highway
    - Big Sur
  - Elephant Seals

There's certainly a quicker way to get from San Francisco to Los Angeles – Interstate 5 is about a six-hour trip – but driving the Pacific Coast Highway (California Route 1) is a bucket list item. I want to warn you – it is a long drive. I don't regret it, but it does wear on you and when you are halfway through the drive, you are ready for it to be over. But, once you commit, there's really not an easy way out!

One special note about the end of our journey. After you drive along the ocean, you leave California Route 1 in Santa Maria and start traveling the rest of the trip to Los Angeles on US 101. Most GPSs might direct you to bypass some of US 101 over the mountains using California Route 154. A nice lady we talked to on this day warned us that because we'd be driving that stretch of road at night, it would be wisest to take just a few extra minutes and stay on US 101, which goes around the mountains.

Henry Cowell Redwoods State Park

We wanted to visit a redwood forest on our trip and chose Henry Cowell Redwoods State Park since it was on the way from our hotel to California Route 1. It was definitely worth the stop! There is a per-vehicle entrance fee and a small visitor center. We walked the loop trail close to the visitor center (less than one mile long) and were mesmerized by the size of the trees. You can touch the trees and get some great pictures.

Carmel Mission

After joining California Route 1, we drove through agricultural lands as we traveled south to Monterey and Carmel-by-the-Sea. We stopped by the Carmel Mission where we took a self-guided tour of the ancient Spanish mission – walking through the old buildings, viewing the neat gardens, and seeing artifacts hundreds of years old.

Pacific Coast Highway

After leaving the mission, we continued south on Route 1 (which is partly named the Pacific Coast Highway). For the first leg of the trip south of Carmel, you are beside the Pacific Ocean, though not really hanging on the side of mountains like you see in pictures of the Pacific Coast Highway. That begins a few miles down the road in Big Sur.

Driving the Pacific Coast Highway is really pretty, and on our day it was also pretty crowded. This part of our vacation was on Saturday – probably not the wisest day for traffic on the Pacific Coast Highway. The entire section of Route 1 that is along the Pacific Ocean is about 120 miles, but your travel speed and stops will make the trip 3 hours or longer.

Big Sur

After driving about 20 miles of Route 1 south of the Carmel Mission, you enter into Big Sur. Big Sur is the general name for the mountainous, forested section of California along the Pacific Coast, halfway between San Francisco and Los Angeles. This is the area that you've likely seen pictures of the highway hugging both the ocean and mountains. It is absolutely stunning and can be a little stressful as you navigate the tight turns and steep drop-offs.

About a year after our trip, a large landslide in Big Sur destroyed part of California Route 1 and temporarily stopped any hope of driving it. Before you make plans to drive the Pacific Coast Highway, ensure that it is completely open.

Other than stopping to take pictures, our only stop in Big Sur was at McWay Waterfall in Pfeiffer Big Sur State Park. The area has a parking lot with restrooms. You hike a very short hike to view a waterfall that flows over the side of the hill and onto the ocean below. It was really pretty and made for a good break while driving along the highway.

Farther down the road (past Big Sur) is the famous Hearst Castle. We didn't stop (it's pretty expensive), but I know it is a popular tourist destination.

Elephant Seals

This was a fairly unexpected part of our day. As we were driving down Route 1, well past Big Sur and near San Simeon, CA, we saw a sign and pull-off for elephant seals. We got out and were pleasantly surprised. Dozens of adult elephant seals were lying on the beach molting (shedding their skin). They were huge animals – several feet long and weighing over 1,000 pounds. We got to watch them from a safe boardwalk – it was a welcome break after stressful hours of driving.

Day 8 Stats

386 miles

Breakfast – hotel

Lunch – In-N-Out Burger (Seaside, CA)

Supper – various fast food after the Pacific Coast Highway

Hotel – Hyatt Regency Westlake (Westlake Village, CA)

Our Route –
    I-680 south to become I-280

A Short and Sweet Introduction to the Great American West Vacation

I-280 west to California Route 17
California 17 south to Mt Hermon Rd.
Mt. Hermon Rd. north (west) to California Route 9
California 9 south to N Big Trees Park Rd. (Henry Cowell State Park entrance)
After the park, continue on California 9 south to California Route 1
California Route 1 (Pacific Coast Highway) south to US 101 in San Luis Obispo, CA
US 101 south to Westlake Village, CA

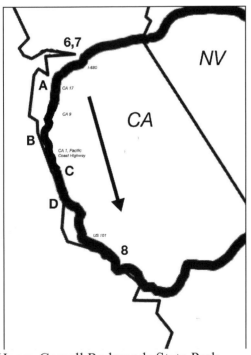

A – Henry Cowell Redwoods State Park
B – Carmel Mission
C – Big Sur
D – Elephant Seals
6,7 – Nights 6 and 7 in Dublin, CA
8 – Night 8 in Westlake Village, CA

Day 9 – Los Angeles (100 miles)

- Hollywood and Tour
- Newport Beach
- Downtown Disney

We had about a half-hour drive to Hollywood from our hotel. This day was Sunday, so traffic was actually pretty manageable. I'm certain that if this was a weekday then we would have easily had twice as long of a drive.

Hollywood and Tour

We actually parked right at the Dolby Theatre where the Academy Awards are given. There is a nice shopping center attached, as well as the famous TLC Chinese Theatre (footprints and handprints). Jimmy Kimmel Live! tapes across the road and there are stars with names in them in the sidewalks all around.

I researched several Hollywood tours and opted to go with a private tour that I found on Groupon. Unlike our Groupon experience in San Francisco, this tour was awesome! The guy's name was David and his tour was called LAdventure Tour. I totally recommend it if he's still doing it. With the Groupon it was really affordable for us and he emailed me in advance of the tour to find out what we wanted to see. I told him who was in our party and he did a good job of taking us to places that we wanted to see and a lot of places that we didn't know about. We saw homes and sights in Hollywood, Beverly Hills, and Bel Air.

Newport Beach

After our tour, we hit the road to go to Newport Beach. By now, traffic was picking up (even on Sunday). Once we hit the beach area, it was crazy. It was VERY difficult to find a parking spot. Going to the beach might be a smart thing to do in Los Angeles on a weekday instead of the weekend.

We wanted to go on a whale watching boat trip in addition to take our kids to the beach. I bought a Groupon for a whale watching trip and we had a couple of hours to kill before our scheduled time. So, while I tried to park (for over an hour), my family went and played in the ocean. We all grabbed lunch from one of the many spots to eat along the beach and then went on our whale watching tour.

I hate to judge all whale watching tours based on ours, but we didn't see any whales. I read this might happen because July isn't a peak time to see whales near Los Angeles. Regardless, we saw a handful of dolphins while out to sea, as well as seals on the way back. It was neat to say we were in a boat in the Pacific Ocean, although we were happy when it was over.

Downtown Disney

Since our hotel was beside Disneyland and since we were looking for a place to meet some old friends for dinner, we chose to meet at Downtown Disney. Downtown Disney is a free shopping and restaurant destination attached to Disneyland and California Adventure Park. There is no admission price and you can walk to it from the hotels on the east side of Disneyland – you just have to walk through park security (no ticket required).

Day 9 Stats

100 miles

Breakfast – hotel

Visit *www.shortandsweetintroductions.com/westlinks* for websites and resources

Lunch – various places in Newport Beach

Supper – in Downtown Disney (with local friends)

Hotel – Best Western Plus Anaheim Inn (Anaheim, CA) – literally across the road from Disneyland and California Adventure Park

Our Route –

    US 101 south to exit 7 in Hollywood
    US 101 south to I-110
    I-110 south to I-405
    I-405 east (south) to California Route 73 (exit 10)
    California 73 south to California 55 (exit 77A)
    California 55 southwest to Newport Beach, CA
    California 55 back northeast to I-5
    I-5 north to Disney Way (exit 109)

Day 10 – Disney California Adventure Park (0 miles)

First, a disclaimer: our family had just been to Disney World in Florida six months earlier and we had been to Disney World a couple of times before that. So, in California we chose Disney California Adventure Park over Disneyland on purpose – it had some similar rides that we liked from Disney World and a few things that we hadn't seen before. If you've never been to Disneyland, then you might choose it over California Adventure. In fact, this day might not appeal to you at all and you might find other things to do (read the next honorable mention for suggestions).

If you've ever been to Disney World in Florida, then you will be struck by how Disneyland and California Adventure are literally right in the middle of Anaheim. In fact, our hotel was right across the street from California Adventure. We walked on the sidewalk to a crosswalk, crossed the road, and took the walkway to the front entrance. It was very convenient. Later in the evening we wanted to change our clothes and it was very easy to get back to the hotel and didn't take too much time.

While Disneyland is similar to Magic Kingdom in Florida and other Disneyland parks around the world, California Adventure is a separate park with some unique rides and other rides you can find at other Disney parks. Among its highlights are Cars Land and its major ride, Radiator Springs Racers. Incredicoaster is a major rollercoaster with an upside-down loop. There is an excellent Frozen stage show. Toy Story Midway Mania and Soarin' Over California are like their Florida counterparts. Grizzly River Run is a neat whitewater rafting ride.

At night, California Adventure puts on the neat show, World of Color. Using water, lights, and special effects, the show occurs in the large lake at the back of the park. Beware, if you stand too close, then you might get wet!

<u>Day 10 Stats</u>

0 miles

Breakfast – hotel

Lunch – in Disney California Adventure Park

Supper – in Disney California Adventure Park

Hotel – Best Western Plus Anaheim Inn (Anaheim, CA) – literally across the road from Disneyland and California Adventure Park

Our Route –

    Walk across the road to Disney California Adventure Park

Honorable Mention – More Los Angeles and San Diego

- Attractions in Los Angeles
- National Parks
- Attractions in San Diego

Like so many other places we visited, we could have easily made a complete vacation just by visiting Los Angeles. Add to that San Diego just a couple of hours south, and there are a lot of things you can do in addition to what we did. This isn't a travel guide for L.A. or San Diego, but here is an overview of some things you might consider.

Attractions in Los Angeles

*a variety of beaches

*Disneyland, California Adventure

*Universal Studios

*Knott's Berry Farm – theme park

*Griffith Observatory – view of L.A. and stargazing

*Getty Center – art museum

*Skyspace L.A. – downtown skyscraper observatory and outdoor glass slide

*La Brea Tar Pits – active fossil site with a fossil museum

*California Science Center – includes one of the space shuttles

*movie studio tours

Visit *www.shortandsweetintroductions.com/westlinks* for websites and resources

National Parks

There are five national parks within 3-6 hours of Los Angeles.

*Joshua Tree National Park – highlighting deserts

*Sequoia National Park – some of the world's largest trees in the mountains

*Kings Canyon National Park – large mountains, a huge canyon, and more sequoia trees

*Death Valley National Park – the lowest elevation in the United States

*Yosemite National Park – beautiful mountain cliffs and some sequoia trees

Attractions in San Diego

*San Diego Zoo

*Legoland (north of San Diego)

*SeaWorld

*various beaches

*Gaslamp District – restaurants, nightspots and more

*Maritime Museum – tour old boats

Day 11 – Driving and Las Vegas (270 miles)

- **Las Vegas**

We got up decently early in the morning and hit the road for Las Vegas. After about an hour of driving through L.A., we spent the next three hours in the desert. It is not a very exciting drive!

Las Vegas

Our goal for Las Vegas was to walk around and see the resorts. Here are some things we learned:

We brought our kids (who were 12 and 9 years old), and we didn't really know if Las Vegas would be a questionable place for them. So, we figured that walking around during the day would be OK. Mostly that was true, but we quickly found out that it is quite unbearable to walk around Vegas in the summer during the day. It is so hot – even with many resorts connected – that you really get drained by the heat every time you walk outside.

So, we decided to take our kids to the hotel pool. For some reason our pool at New York, New York closed at 7:00 PM. I don't know if all Vegas pools are like that, but that meant that we changed our clothes to go swimming, and then did zero swimming.

Next, we decided to go out after sunset to try to see a few sights. BAD IDEA!!! Las Vegas after sunset is no place for kids. We didn't make it very far before we figured that out and quickly ended our night.

So, whatever your plans are for Las Vegas, keep our experiences in mind if you have kids. My wife and I would like to go back – the resorts are magnificent and we would love to see some shows. However, we won't be going back with our kids!

Day 11 Stats

270 miles

Breakfast – hotel

Lunch – fast food in Las Vegas

Supper – in our hotel – New York, New York

Hotel – New York, New York (Las Vegas, NV)

Our Route –

    I-5 south to California Route 22
    California 22 east to California Route 55
    California 55 north to California Route 91
    California 91 east to I-15
    I-15 north to Las Vegas

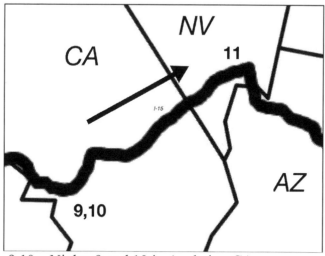

9,10 – Nights 9 and 10 in Anaheim, CA
11 – Night 11 in Las Vegas, NV

Day 12 – Driving and Grand Canyon (554 miles)

- Hoover Dam
- Grand Canyon National Park
- Four Corners Monument

While we still had three days of vacation left, I have to admit that we were kind of getting over the two-week vacation by this point. We had a lot of driving to do in addition to our remaining destinations. Today's long day of driving mixed in with our weariness led to us not giving today's destinations their just due. But, here is what we did and an overview of what you can do.

Hoover Dam

Helping to provide water and electricity to millions, the Hoover Dam is an engineering marvel just outside of Las Vegas. Not too long ago you would actually drive over the dam to continue into Arizona. Today they have bypassed the dam with a nearby bridge. While you can see the bridge from the dam, you can't see the dam from the bridge – that is quite disappointing!

There is a fee for just about everything at Hoover Dam – a fee to park, a fee for the tour, and even a fee to go in the visitor center. You can walk onto the observation deck for free, but that's after you've paid to park. We didn't take the time do the tour or the visitor center, though I took a tour when I was a kid. I really wish we had time to do this with our family because I was impressed with the tour years ago. There are two tour options – one just goes through the powerplant, while the other tour adds a trip into the dam itself.

Visit *www.shortandsweetintroductions.com/westlinks* for websites and resources

Grand Canyon National Park

After Smoky Mountain National Park in the eastern United States, Grand Canyon National Park is the second-most visited national park in the U.S. Just typing that line brings me guilt because of how quickly we saw it. With a depth over one mile, a width of up to 18 miles across, and a length over 200 miles long, Grand Canyon is quite large and a little overwhelming.

There are two sides to the Grand Canyon – the North Rim and the South Rim – and they are both in the park. The South Rim is more easily accessed from major cities, airports, and Interstate 40. It is also open year-round, while the North Rim is not. Keep in mind that while the two rims are literally only miles apart, it can take nearly four hours to drive from one side to the other!

Like many people, we visited the South Rim. Most people start their visit in Grand Canyon Village. Here you can visit the visitor center, general store, lodges, and restaurants; and you can see neat views. While many roads are accessible by cars, some roads are only accessible by park shuttle buses. In fact, even with a car, it might be easier to see many of the vistas by using the shuttle buses.

Some of the most popular attractions in Grand Canyon include hikes into the canyon, mule trips, and river raft rides. The mule trips and river raft rides book months in advance – keep that in mind when you are planning your trip.

Another popular attraction associated with the Grand Canyon is the Grand Canyon Skywalk. Opened in 2007, the Grand Canyon Skywalk is a glass walkway over a portion of the canyon. The Skywalk is not in Grand Canyon National Park, but rather operated by the Hualapai Tribe. As such, it is a long way from Grand Canyon Village and national park passes will not grant you free admission to the Skywalk. (Actually, the

Grand Canyon Skywalk is only about 2½ hours from Las Vegas, while it is nearly 5 hours from Grand Canyon Village!)

Four Corners Monument

The Four Corners Monument is the point where Utah, Colorado, Arizona, and New Mexico all meet. It is the only location in the United States where four states come together in one place. It is located on Navajo land and run by the Navajo Nation. There is a small admission fee and a small visitor center open year-round.

Please note that the monument is not open 24 hours. We had hoped to see it when we drove through on our way to our hotel in Cortez, CO. Unfortunately, it was closed when we came through at night and we were not able to see it.

Day 12 Stats

554 miles

Breakfast – hotel

Lunch – a local restaurant in Williams, AZ along the historic Route 66

Supper – fast food along US 160 in Arizona

Hotel – White Eagle Inn and Lodge (Cortez, CO)

Our Route –

    I-515 southeast to US 93
    US 93 south (past Hoover Dam) to I-40
    I-40 east to Arizona Route 64 (exit 165)
    Arizona 64 north to Grand Canyon, then east to US 89
    US 89 north to US 160
    US 160 east to Cortez, CO

Visit *www.shortandsweetintroductions.com/westlinks* for websites and resources

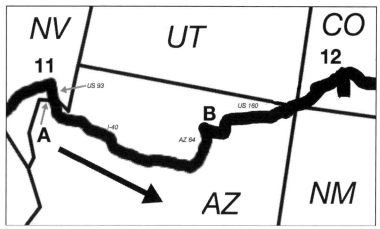

A – Hoover Dam
B – Grand Canyon National Park
11 – Night 11 in Las Vegas, NV
12 – Night 12 in Cortez, CO

A Short and Sweet Introduction to the Great American West Vacation

Honorable Mention – Alternate Route Home through Canyonlands and Arches

When planning our trip, I considered three options to go home. The first option was to leave the Grand Canyon and simply continue east on Interstate 40 – heading back home. That wasn't ambitious enough, so the other two options were either 1) going through Mesa Verde and Great Sand Dunes or 2) going through Canyonlands National Park and Arches National Park.

We chose the Mesa Verde and Great Sand Dunes option – it seemed like it fit best into our schedule and I decided that Mesa Verde would be a truly unique sight. Pictures of Canyonlands and Arches are absolutely beautiful and I would really love to see them some day. But, this was a trip where we had to prioritize the sights that we saw, understanding that we couldn't possibly see everything.

But, if you decide to take the route to Canyonlands and Arches, then after leaving the Grand Canyon on US 160, you will turn north onto US 191. US 191 goes right between Canyonlands National Park on the west and Arches National Park on the east – the roads that go to each park are actually less than six miles apart on US 191.

After visiting both parks, you will continue on US 191 north to Interstate 70 and then begin your trip back east. Interstate 70 travels through the heart of Colorado and the Rocky Mountains, including through or nearby some of Colorado's premiere skiing destinations – and then through Denver.

Day 13 – Mesa Verde and Driving (608 miles)

- Mesa Verde National Park
- Great Sand Dunes National Park and Preserve

We probably bit off a little more than we could chew for this day. We had every intention of driving over 600 miles, visiting Mesa Verde, and visiting Great Sand Dunes National Park and Preserve. By the time we got to the road to go to the Great Sand Dunes, we just couldn't do it. It was Day 13 and we were tired. I'm sure it is beautiful and we were able to see it rising in the distance, but we decided we had enough and just wanted to keep heading home.

Mesa Verde National Park

Our morning started at Mesa Verde National Park. It is home to magnificent dwellings carved into the side of the mountains by the Pueblo Indians. A spectacular sight, the dwellings are over 1,000 years old and contain hundreds of different rooms.

The dwellings are several miles into the park and access to the park is one way in and one way out. That means that you need to set aside 2-3 hours of time even if you just want to take a few pictures. Tours are available where you can actually hike through some of the dwellings. Some tours are self-guided and others require tickets. Ticketed tours aren't expensive but can only be purchased up to two days in advance. You can purchase tickets at both the Chapin Mesa Archeological Museum (by the dwellings) and at the Visitor and Research Center (located at the park entrance – not by the dwellings). Though you can get tickets at both locations, the park website says that you have a better chance of getting reservations at the Visitor and Research Center.

We drove Mesa Top Ruins Rd. to the Chapin Mesa Archaeological Museum and then drove one of the two loop roads just past the museum. There are pull-off parking lots for views of the dwellings. Mesa Verde does have a seasonal lodge and seasonal campground, as well as restaurant options.

Great Sand Dunes National Park and Preserve

OK, full disclaimer – we didn't go here. We saw it from the distance, but decided we were too tired and going to get to the hotel too late. The Great Sand Dunes wasn't super close to our route – though I estimated that it would only take about an extra half hour of driving.

The Great Sand Dunes are basically mountains of sand – extending several hundreds of feet above the land around them. In addition to the visitor center, people will hike in the dunes and even sandboard and sand sled down the dunes! The park has a lodge, cabins, and camping, as well as a restaurant.

Day 13 Stats

608 miles

Breakfast – hotel

Lunch – local restaurant in Pagosa Springs, CO

Supper – Pizza Hut in La Junta, CO

Hotel – Kansas Country Inn (Oakley, KS)

Our Route –

>US 160 east to Mesa Verde, then after the park continue east to become Colorado Route 10
>Colorado 10 east to Colorado Route 109
>Colorado 109 north to east on County Rd. 808, to north on Rd. 31, to Colorado Route 96

Colorado 96 east to US 287
US 287 north to US 40
US 40 east to Oakley, KS

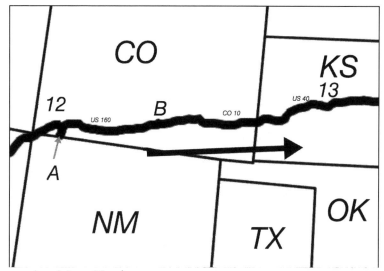

A – Mesa Verde
B – Great Sand Dunes National Park
12 – Night 12 in Cortez, CO
13 – Night 13 in Oakley, KS

Day 14 – Drive, Drive, Drive (859 miles)

I wish I could say that we saw something cool on this day, but we didn't. It was our farthest distance to travel in one day and it was quite a trip! I drove the first leg of the trip and since everyone was exhausted and sleeping, I drove nearly four hours without stopping. It seemed like a great idea and helped us make great time, but I paid with a terrible leg pain the next few weeks!

I guess that this is a good time to point out that this trip totaled nearly 6,000 miles and you need to be mindful of your health. Make sure that you take time to walk when you stop. Make sure that you adjust your sitting position as you travel.

We stopped for lunch in Kansas City and supper in St. Louis. Our biggest mistake was that we ate supper before we made it through St. Louis instead of after. So, that put us trying to get through St. Louis at rush hour instead of probably making it through right before rush hour. Keep things like this in mind when you travel through major cities.

I'm so glad that we took this trip. Although we saw so many great things, I really enjoyed the variety of scenery that we saw by driving instead of flying. I rarely get to drive through mountains and deserts.

We drove some places that I will probably never drive again. Life is only so long and there is so much to see. There's a decent chance I'll see Yellowstone again and even San Francisco again, but I'll probably never drive from one to the other again. Similarly, I'll probably revisit Los Angeles, but never again drive the Pacific Coast Highway there from San Francisco.

I'll probably never drive through southwest Colorado near Mesa Verde again. I may never again drive up a mountain from Reno and descend into Lake Tahoe. So much of this trip was once-in-a-lifetime.

Thankfully, on this day, we left early enough that we arrived home before midnight. We were tired and happy to be home. The first thing we did was go to the grocery store to get milk. And of course, we really enjoyed sleeping in our own beds!

Day 14 Stats

859 miles

Breakfast – hotel

Lunch – fast food in Kansas City

Supper – Golden Corral in St. Louis (it was my daughter's birthday and she wanted all-you-can eat steak!)

Our Route –

    I-70 west to home

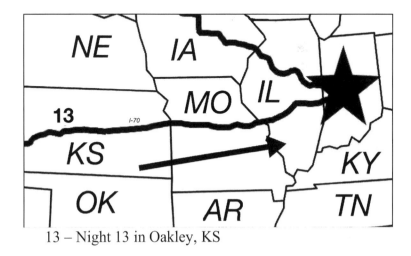

13 – Night 13 in Oakley, KS

OTHER THINGS

Visit *www.shortandsweetintroductions.com/westlinks* for websites and resources

A Word about Lodging

If you've traveled the midwestern, eastern, or southern United States, then you are used to a wide variety of lodging options just about everywhere you go. You usually have no problem finding chain hotels, mom-and-pop motels, and expensive hotels and resorts. As you travel out west, however, it might be much harder to find exactly what you're used to.

There are many places where high-end hotels just don't exist. In fact, even western U.S. chain motels might be outdated and not exactly somewhere you'd stay elsewhere. The national park lodges, while expensive and in high demand, aren't usually high-end hotels either.

The best thing you can do is read ratings online. Use other peoples' experiences (with a grain of salt) and online pictures to determine where you are going to stay. Use Google Street View to look at the hotel's surroundings – what buildings are nearby and does it look like an area you feel safe staying in?

While some of you are "figure it out as you go" vacation people, keep in mind that without planning your lodging in advance, you might be staying in the most interesting motel rooms of your life. Furthermore, if you travel west during the summer like so many other people, you might have trouble finding places to stay at all.

The same thing goes for campgrounds. Do your research in advance and don't assume that you'll always find a place to stay!

Time of Year

If you plan to do the trip that we did, then the time of year you travel is somewhat limited. The biggest problem is Yellowstone – some parts of Grand Loop Rd. are closed because of snow beginning in October and don't open again until May!

A lot of people travel during the hot summer months because of summer break from school. If that is when you must travel, then planning your trip for the beginning or end of your summer break is best. If you don't have to plan your trip around a school summer break, then it is wisest to take your great American west vacation in May or September. Summer crowds mean that park roads are busier, lodging reservations are harder to come by, and restaurant lines will be longer.

Regardless of the time of year, you have to pack for a variety of temperatures. Our vacation was during the first two weeks of July, and we spent more time being cold than we expected. We were underprepared to keep warm in Yellowstone and San Francisco. For that matter, our trip down the Pacific Coast Highway was chilly as well. On the other hand, Los Angeles was warm and Las Vegas was miserably hot!

If you have the opportunity to do the desert southwest portion of this trip outside of the summer, then it might be worth it to wait. The average high in Las Vegas in January is 60 degrees Fahrenheit, while the average high in July is 105!

Visit *www.shortandsweetintroductions.com/westlinks* for websites and resources

Animals We Saw on Our Trip

Bighorn Sheep (Badlands – Day 2)

Bison (Badlands – Day 2, Yellowstone – Day 4)

Black Bear (Yellowstone – Day 4)

Coyote (Yellowstone – Day 5)

Dolphin (Newport Beach, CA – Day 9)

Elephant Seal (San Simeon, CA – Day 8)

Elk (Black Hills – Day 2, Yellowstone – Day 4, Gardiner, MT – Day 4)

Mule Deer (Devil's Tower – Day 3, Mesa Verde – Day 13)

Prairie Dog (Badlands – Day 2, Devil's Tower – Day 3)

Pronghorn (Badlands – Day 2)

Seal (Newport Beach, CA – Day 9)

Other American West Trips

The purpose of this book isn't to tell you everything you can do in the western United States – I haven't even been able to touch on everything to do at the destinations that we visited. However, here are a few other vacations that you could take to visit other areas of the western U.S. besides the places I already mentioned in this book.

Utah and Colorado

I've known people who have made their entire vacation a loop through Utah and Colorado. There are places in Utah that I've already given honorable mentions to: Salt Lake City, Zion National Park, Arches National Park, and Canyonlands National Park. In addition, you can visit Lake Powell, Monument Valley, Grand Staircase-Escalante National Monument, and Capitol Reef National Park. In Colorado, visit Pike's Peak, Garden of the Gods, Dinosaur National Monument, Black Canyon of the Gunnison National Park, and Rocky Mountain National Park – in addition to Mesa Verde and Great Sand Dunes National Park. This list doesn't even include the mountain resort towns in both Utah and Colorado.

Washington and Oregon

I've never been here, so I don't want to act like an expert about these states. I know that if I ever get to visit, then I will want to see Mt. St. Helens, Olympic National Park, Seattle, Portland, the Columbia River Gorge, and probably a side trip to Vancouver, Canada.

Visit *www.shortandsweetintroductions.com/westlinks* for websites and resources

Other Resources

Remember, this is just an introduction to the great American west. On my website, I've included links to extra resources that might help you plan your trip.

I've included links to the websites of all of the national parks, memorials, and other attractions mentioned in this book.

I've included links to all of the hotels that we stayed at.

I've included links to books that will help you go more in-depth about various sights.

*Visit **www.shortandsweetintroductions.com/westlinks** for links to all of these resources.*

Did you enjoy this book? If so, then please leave a review wherever you purchased it!

Do you have any questions, comments, or suggestions? Contact me at *shortandsweetintroductions.com/contact*

Would you like free previews and updates about future books? Join my email list at *shortandsweetintroductions.com/email*

Visit *www.shortandsweetintroductions.com/westlinks* for websites and resources

About the Author

My name is Joe Dodridge and I live in Fishers, Indiana. My full-time job is a high school teacher. I've taught school for a dozen years and I was a pastor for 10 years. I'm married and we have two children.

I write both travel books and Christian devotionals.

My writing "career" really started in eleventh grade when I wrote that year's first essay for English. My teacher gave me my rough draft back with over half of it crossed out and told me what I wrote was useless. I went on to get a C on that first paper and it was the beginning of a brutal boot camp experience of learning how to properly write. (split infinitive – it's OK!)

After countless papers in college and graduate school, my graduate thesis advisor was the daughter of an English professor and a journal editor. So, I went through boot camp 2.0.

In 2007, I started writing a daily devotional online. I bought a website and wrote over 150 devotionals.

Since then, I've written a lot of things that haven't made it out of my computer until July 2017 when I wrote my first book, ***A Short and Sweet Introduction to Walt Disney World Resort: 2017-2018.*** That book came out of my love for Disney World, my love for travel, and my desire to finally get a book written.

Other Books by Joe Dodridge

250 Tips and Tricks for Walt Disney World Resort (January 2018)

The problem with most tips books is they aren't full of that many tips. This book gives you over 250 tips – no stories about tips, just tips.

Our Kids – Our Responsibility, Months 1-6 "Jesus's Teaching" and *"Genesis"* (January, March 2018)

If you're like our family, you've tried daily devotions and failed. This weekly family devotional goes more in-depth and provides an extra time just for parents. (Separate books of months 1-3 and months 4-6 are also available.)

A Short and Sweet Introduction to Walt Disney World Resort:2018 (February 2018)

Most Disney World guidebooks read like encyclopedias – too much information and not enough introduction. This second edition, 60-page guide book introduces you to the parks, hotels, dining, and more without overwhelming you!

A Short and Sweet Introduction to Indianapolis (March 2018)

Most Indianapolis guidebooks are outdated and don't give a good overview. This book introduces you to things to do, how to get around, and what to see.

Visit *www.shortandsweetintroductions.com/westlinks* for websites and resources

A Disney World Combo Book (March 2018)

This is a combination of my two other Disney World books: *250 Tips and Tricks for Walt Disney World Resort* and *A Short and Sweet Introduction to Walt Disney World Resort: 2018.*

Future Book Projects

A Short and Sweet Introduction to Washington DC

Audiobook versions of my current books

Just For You...

 Join my email list for book updates at shortandsweetintroductions.com/email

 Share this book on Facebook, Twitter, or Instagram.

Made in the USA
Columbia, SC
24 July 2021